W9-BIL-367

LEARN TO DRAW
CARTOONS
A Step-by-Step Guide

EMMETT ELVIN

BACKPACKBOOKS
o
NEW YORK

Copyright © 2004 by Kandour Ltd UK

This 2004 edition published by Backpack Books,
by arrangement with Kandour Ltd UK.

Backpack Books
122 Fifth Avenue
New York, NY 10011

ISBN 0-7607-6556-1

Printed and bound in United Kingdom

04 05 06 07 08 MCH 10 9 8 7 6 5 4 3 2 1

Created by Metro Media Ltd, UK
Author and illustrator: Emmett Elvin
Cover and content design: Eugene Felder, Emmett Elvin
Page layout: Eugene Felder
Managing editors: Emma Hayley, Jenny Ross

CONTENTS

FOREWORD

Some people hate politics. Others hate broccoli. But I have never, *ever* met anyone who hates cartoons. We grow up on them, we watch them for hours at a time, or plunge our heads deep into comic books and cartoon strips. They fascinate and delight us, transporting us from our drab, everyday world directly to the outer reaches of our imagination. And here lies the secret of what makes cartoons so good, exciting, hilarious, stunning, and essential.

You can do what you like.

Yes, you can. Trouble is, we don't always have the skills necessary to do our imaginations justice. Why can't I get that space station orbiting the planet Thrukkitz to look like a space station? Why are hands so hard to draw? Why do my *funny animals* look miserable?

By the time you've worked through this book, you'll be fully equipped to create your own strips, work on your animation ideas, or just have fun drawing your own creations.

I *love* cartoons. I love reading them, watching them, drawing them, and showing other people how it's done.

I'm not so keen on broccoli, though!

Emmett Elvin
Author

section one

introduction

Introduction

What is a cartoon?

The word "cartoon" probably has one of the widest meanings of any word in the English language. It started life as a word for a preliminary sketch an artist would make before attempting a full-blown painting.

But what does it mean now, in the twenty-first century?

Krazy Kat, Doonesbury, Pocahontas, Peanuts, and Princess Mononoke: These are all undisputedly cartoons, but are all hugely different in their scope and subject matter. They all have one thing in common, though. Reality has been subverted. Larger than life, caricature, supercolorful these are the words used to describe cartoons.

Okay, so when is a cartoon not a cartoon?

The two pictures below show Mr. Franklin Q. Krumble having an idea. One is drawn in a realistic style, the other in a cartoon style.

Having trouble telling which is which? I didn't think so.

Shown at left is the reality of a person having an idea. But right is the *idea* of an idea. Cartoons are less concerned with what a thing looks like as much as the idea of the thing. Everything gets reduced to what is at the core of an action, expression, shape, etc.

Cartoons: the ground rules

Keeping this in mind, we can get a clearer idea about what our own approach to cartoons might be. Here are some simple rules:

1. Throw out anything not absolutely necessary.
2. Push what you've got left to the limit.

I could have filled the rest of this page with a slew of other guidelines, but the above are the only two essential ones. Keep them in mind as you work through this book!

Squash, stretch, and snap

The dynamics of things

Take a look at the sequence below. It's a series of drawings you probably recognize from a cartoon of some kind. It represents one of the basic principles of cartoons and animation, namely stretch and squash.

1. First, a regular cartoon ball is dropped from a respectable height.
2. As the ball plummets to the ground, it appears to stretch, due to the effects of cartoon gravity.
3. All the energy is working in a downward direction until the ball comes into contact with the ground.
4. There's nowhere for the energy to go but outward, so the ball begins to expand in that direction.
5. But there is also energy in the ball's own natural shape. So when the outward energy can't expand anymore, it begins to retract back into the shape of a ball.
6. Any energy left in the ball then propels it upwards, causing the "bounce" effect.

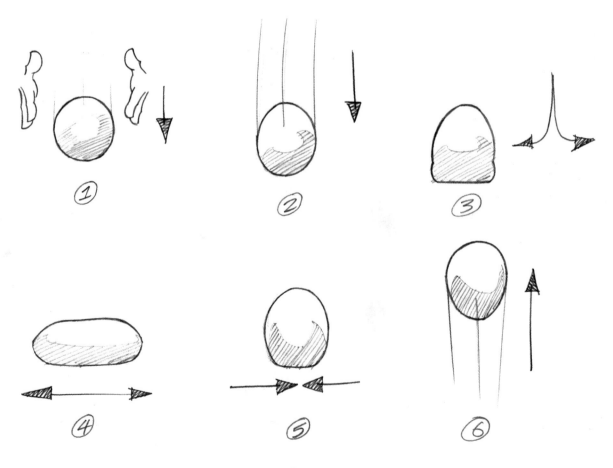

An important other thing

There probably are a few things in the book that you can live without. But this isn't one of them. Understanding the effects of gravity and force, and subsequently distorting them for your own ends, is not only essential, it's also one of the most horn-honkingly fun things about being a cartoonist.

The sequence over the next page shows this in action. But no peeking until you've come to grips with the ball stuff, okay?

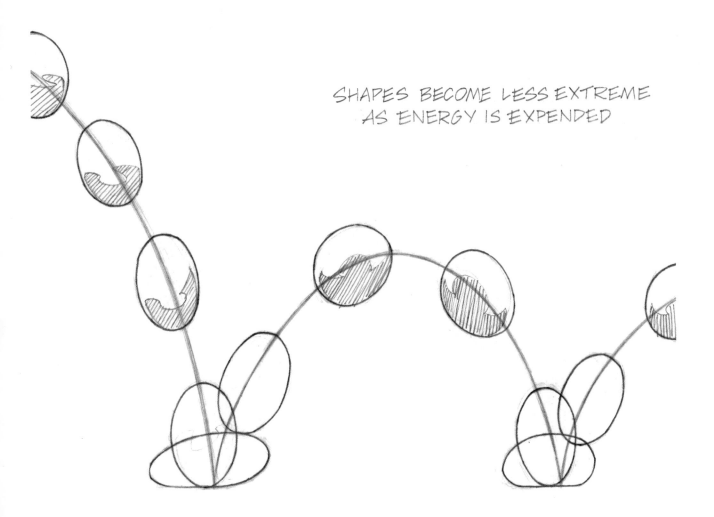

SHAPES BECOME LESS EXTREME
AS ENERGY IS EXPENDED

What you'll need

Pencils

You won't get very far without these. Whether you use a soft or hard pencil is your own personal choice. The "H" pencils are hard and the "B" pencils are soft. I usually "rough" out with a harder pencil and "tighten up" with a softer, darker one. Most pencils you find at your local general store are HBs neither soft nor hard. The full range are available at your local graphic supplies store.

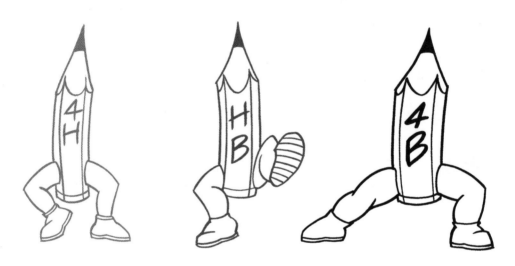

Eraser

You can only do without one of these if you never make mistakes. I go through plenty of erasers. The best ones are putty erasers. They tend to wear out more quickly, but they really clean up like no other type. Try to avoid an eraser that's too rough and tears up the paper.

Sharpener

Electric sharpener, craft blade, it doesn't really matter. What does matter is keeping that pencil sharp. That means keeping whatever blade that sharpens your pencils sharp, too. A blunt blade will wreck your pencil points.

Paper

Some people think copier paper was made for copying machines. No! It was made for artists to have cheap paper to experiment on! Don't waste good paper when you doodle and work out ideas. Many cartoonists use nothing but copier paper.

At the other end of the scale is Bristol paper. This is a heavy, superfine paper, ideally suited to producing slick, highly polished results. For the beginner, though, it's prohibitively expensive. An affordable alternative is a block of cartridge paper.

A bunch of other stuff you might want

Rulers

"You're not allowed to use a ruler here!" I heard this remark once in a studio I was working in. But rulers have their uses in cartoons: for borders of cartoon strips, and for working out difficult perspective (see later in this book). Ruled lines tend to look stiff and lifeless and should generally be avoided.

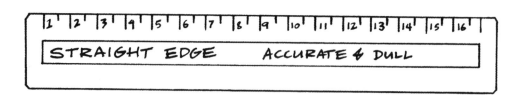

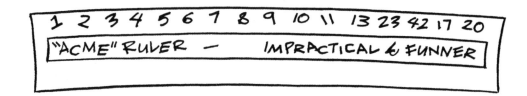

Ink

Happy with your pencil art? Then you may want to make it permanent. India Ink comes in two types permanent and nonpermanent. Get the permanent stuff. The shellac in it makes it waterproof, so once it's dried, it's going nowhere. But what to apply it with?

Brush versus pencil

Most people seem more comfortable starting off with a dip pen when they start to ink. This is probably because it's closer to what they're used to. But for real fluidity and seemless, slick lines, you'll want to come to grips with a brush. This is one area where it really pays to spend some money. A cheap, lousy brush will just hold you back and frustrate you. Try starting with a number one or two brush. It doesn't have to be made of the finest Russian sable; a synthetic fiber brush should be fine (and a whole lot cheaper). What you must remember to do is ALWAYS clean out your brush thoroughly when you're done. Otherwise it will quickly become utterly useless. Forgetfulness can be expensive.

Marker pen

You can get some great results with a marker pen. Not the skinny little ones you might write your name with, but the ones you'd use to write signs with. Although they are very unforgiving, they can be surprisingly expressive. See later on for some examples.

How do I hold a pencil?

Getting a grip

You never hear this question, largely because everyone assumes they know how to hold a pencil. They probably *do,* at least as far as writing their name is concerned. Have a look at the two drawings below.

A.

B.

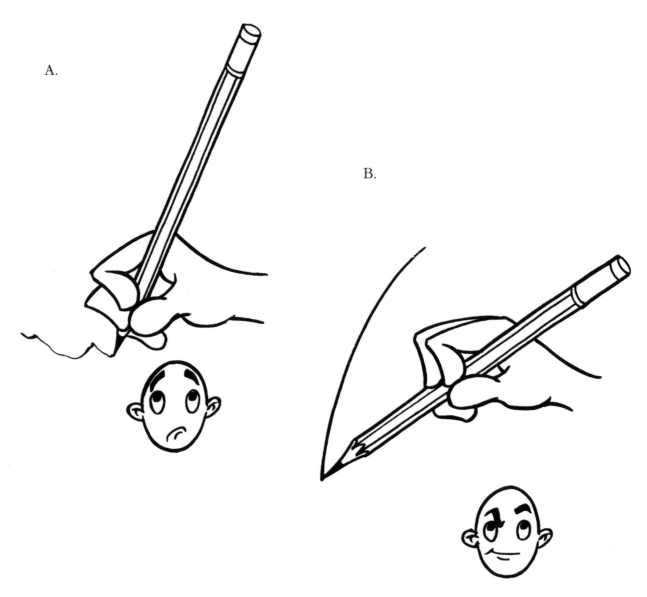

Which way would you hold the pencil to draw? If your answer is A, why not try it the other way? You might find it strange at first, but I guarantee your line will become more expressive. Plus, you'll be able to draw curved lines far more easily.

Use your wrist

If we use the length of the pencil, rather than just the tip, we can use the natural "swing" of our wrist, or even elbow, to create big sweeping lines. The great thing is we don't even have to think about it. Just get your hand positioned in the right place and let the natural swing of your wrist create the curve.

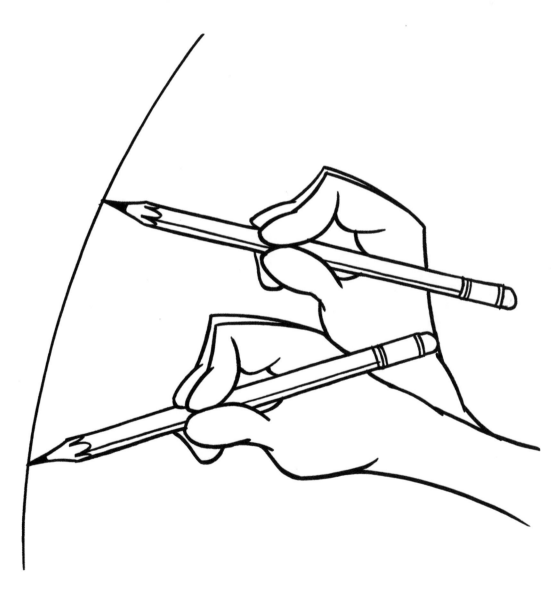

Okay, okay, enough of the lecture. The next chapter is where we start to get a grip on the meat of the matter. Namely, drawing bodies.

section two

bodies

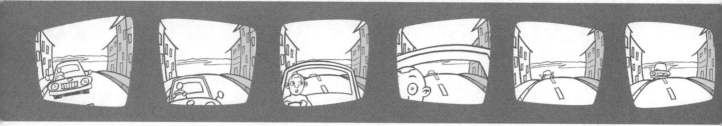

Body types

Skinny, tubby, big, small, brainy, and dumb

Have a good look at your favorite cartoon show. See the variety of shapes and sizes of the characters? From Tom and Jerry to Ren & Stimpy to Pinky and the Brain, differences in shape and size have always been used to emphasize character. Big is often stupid. Small is often smart. These aren't rules, just tendencies that cartoons frequently follow. Do we want people to sympathize with our character? Then we make them vulnerable.

Below are a bunch of different character types. I've deliberately left off any expressions or detail to show what can be communicated purely by body type.

Why you, I oughta . . .

Below is a typically big, strong cartoon character. What makes him physically different from his fellow cartoon types?

– WIDE SHOULDERS
– "V" SHAPE CHEST
– SHORTER LEGS

The broad shoulders and chest communicate brawn and physical confidence. By making his legs shorter than might be normal, we emphasize his upper body. Plus, it lends his overly macho physique a sense of the ridiculous.

When drawing a human figure, we should keep the head size quite small. Bigger, taller people have larger bodies, but their heads are just the same size as anyone else's.

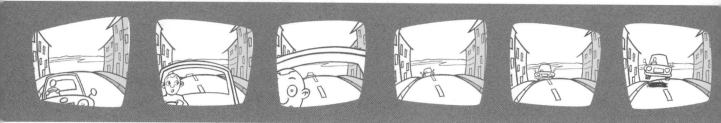

Don't hit me!

All the main ideas from the big, powerful character on the previous page can be turned inside-out to produce a weedy, unthreatening one:

— NARROW SHOULDERS
— NARROW CHEST
— SKINNY NECK

The teenage character at above left has quite a skeletal form, while the feline figure manages to look more cute. Fur, size, and a tummy certainly help to achieve this.

Head size is also much bigger in relation to the body, and posture will generally be far less threatening than with powerful characters.

Boys versus girls

Angular or curvaceous

Below is a simple comparison of male cartoon shapes versus female ones. It's best to start off by thinking in terms of the underlying structure.

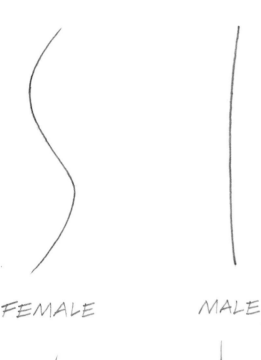

FEMALE   MALE

If the first two drawings to the left don't get the point across, the two underneath should. Femininity is all about curve. Conversely, masculinity is much more hard-edged.

It's always a good idea to think before we draw. And what we should be thinking is: "What is at the essence of what we're trying to draw?"

A good cartoon is not just the surface detail. If we understand the essence, this dictates the structure. What we do with that structure produces the final drawing.

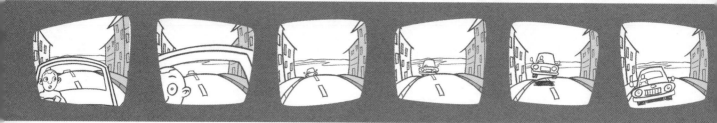

Basic body building

Anatomy of a cartoon

Below is everything you need to put a basic cartoon body together. You can change the shape of any of the components, and even do away with some of them completely! But with this as your framework, you'll be able to draw humans, funny animals, Martians, and plenty more besides.

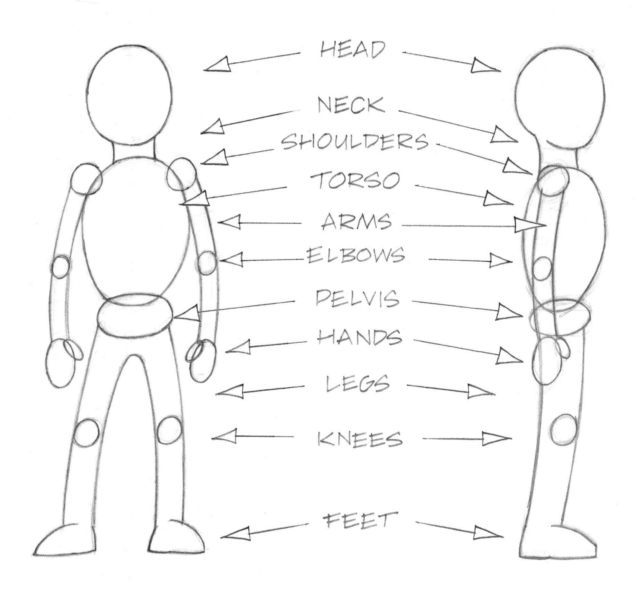

Before we add any more detail to our basic body, let's see what we can do with just this basic framework.

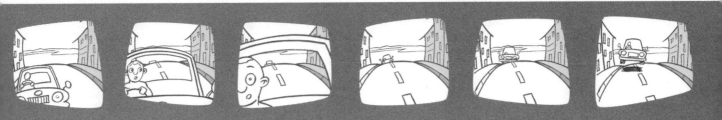

What's your angle?

Let's look at what happens to the various components when we move a body around. To keep it simple, let's look at just the torso and shoulders from three different angles.

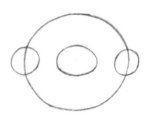

Here's what happens when we do the same thing with the whole body.

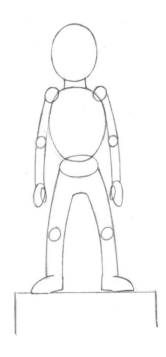
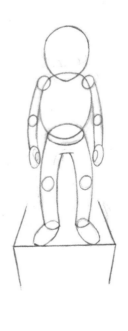
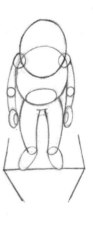

Notice how the various parts not only change position but also change their shape.

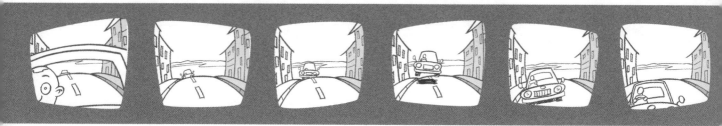

Lines of action

Something to hang your body on

When we want to draw a body in a certain position or action, we start by indicating its general dynamics. We do this by using lines of action. In the drawings below, you can see how once the general position is established, we then "hang" the body on the line.

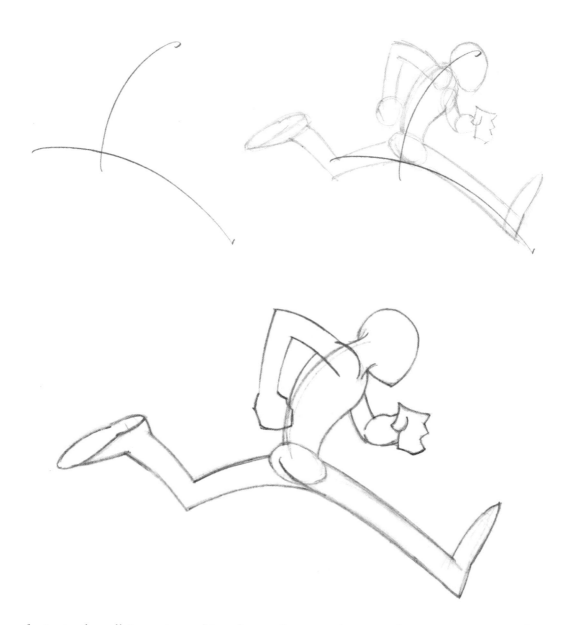

The *shape* is the all-important thing here. Once we've got that, we use it to dictate the shape of the body parts.

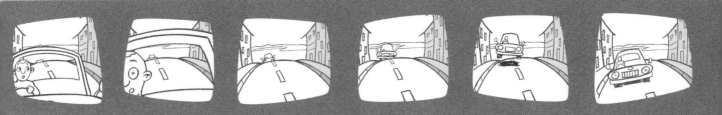

More lines of action

Drawing the female character

Draw from the hip

Let's take what we've learned so far to help us draw a curvaceous girl. We'll start by getting the line of action right. For this drawing, it's a pulled-out "S" shape. The center of this line will represent the spine, with the head and legs following the rest of the shape, as below.

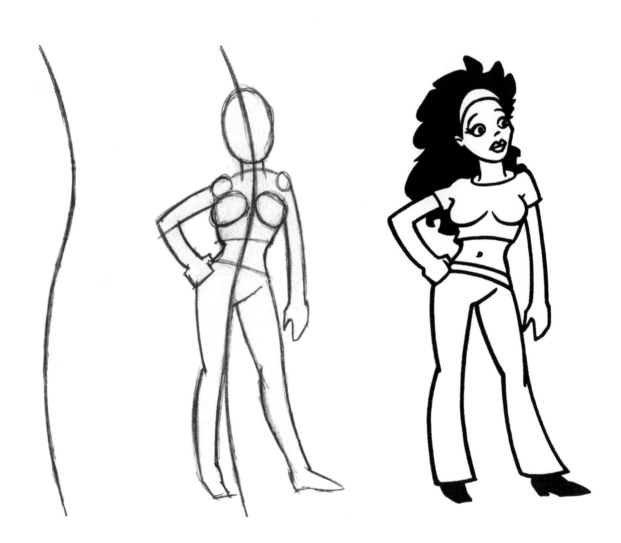

The next thing we do is establish where the hips and shoulders will be. See how the hips and shoulders remain at a right angle to the curve? They do this no matter what kind of line of action you use. Notice also the hip line and shoulder line are going in different directions. Because the hip line is higher on her left side, this means her left leg must be straighter. This in turn means this is the leg carrying most of the weight.

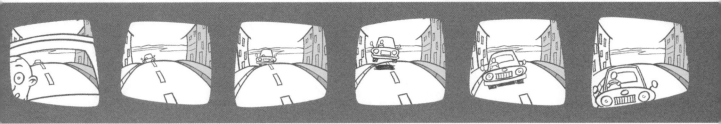

Beauty and ink

Once the basic components are in place, we can work on the surface detail. Don't worry too much about her face at this point. There's plenty about that coming up in the next chapter.

Remember, females have slimmer necks and waists than males, and their hands and feet are smaller.

On the right is the same girl, but this time drawn from behind. See if you can work out where the line of action is in this drawing. Try straightening out the line of action. What effect will this have on the final drawing?

Drawing male characters

As I mentioned earlier in the chapter, cartoon males tend to be more angular and less curvy. Let's start with a much straighter line of action and build from there.

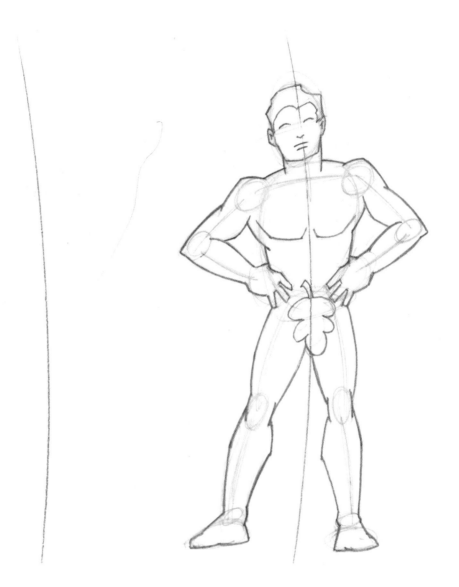

Start by putting in the shoulder and hip positions, and build the rest of the body on that framework. Cartoon guys have wider shoulders, are less "leggy," and have heavier necks. If we want a real macho type, give him a big, deep chin, and a "V" chest.

Rear view and silliness

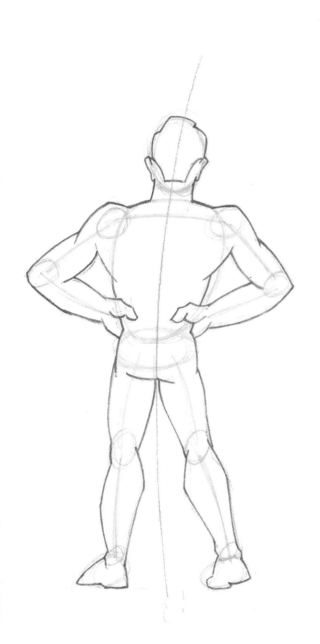

Nonhuman bodies

Animals, funny or otherwise

Now let's turn our attention to those mainstays of cartoons the "funny animal" types. Most of the differences here are superficial ones, meaning their underlying structure is much the same. So what are the superficial differences?

 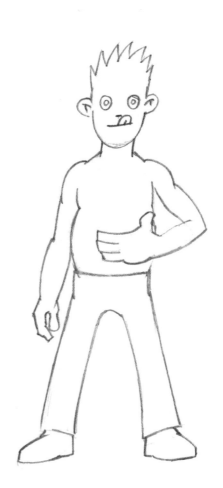

Aside from the differences above, the most obvious is height. This doesn't mean just the size of the drawing. It's to do with the head to height ratio. All characters have them so we may as well learn something about this.

We'll have an in-depth look at the creation of a nonhuman character in a later chapter.

Comparisons

As the picture below shows, the head sizes on these characters are all exactly the same. It's the ratio between body and head that's different. This has a pretty dramatic effect on the kind of character we produce. At two heads high we have the cutest. It probably looks that way because this is the ratio that most closely resembles a baby's.

At the other end of the scale we have the biggest, most threatening-looking character. His massive body says "power." And it's not just because he's taller than the others. His head is tiny compared with his body. This is just as it would be if we met an eight-feet-tall person.

Four heads high is the most standard for a funny animal cartoon character. Six heads high is pretty close to a teenager's proportions. A fully grown six-foot male is approximately seven heads high.

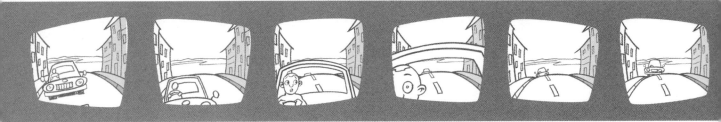

Body do's and don'ts

Frequently made mistakes

At the back of this book are numerous reference poses of bodies in motion. But to round off this chapter, let's have a quick peek at where it can all go horribly wrong.

SPINE CURVE GOOD – BODY LOOKS RELAXED

LINE OF ACTION TOO STRAIGHT – BODY LOOKS STIFF

LINE OF ACTION IN WRONG DIRECTION!

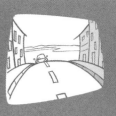

Head, neck, and weight

THE NECK SHOULD
"FLOW" INTO HEAD
& SHOULDERS

WAY TOO STRAIGHT

MORE LIKE IT

WEIGHT

THIS FIGURE HAS ITS
WEIGHT BADLY DISTRIBUTED–

THE LEGS AND PELVIS
ARE NOT SUPPORTING
THE UPPER BODY
PROPERLY

section three

heads, hands, and feet

Heads

Humans

As human heads are generally simpler, at least in cartoons, they seem a good place to start. At the end of this section you should be able to draw a human head from any angle.

Let's get busy with the basics.

A cartoon head can be almost any shape we like. Even triangular or cone-shaped. But before we get too carried away we should learn the construction of a head that's a little closer to home.

This means working with a roughly egg-shaped oval.

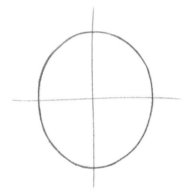

1. Draw the oval and divide it in half, lengthwise, and top to bottom.

2. Add the eyes on the center line.

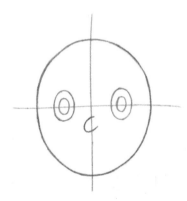

3. Put the ears just below the center line, the nose in the center and the mouth roughly central.

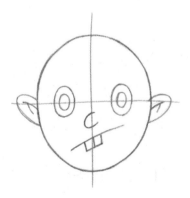

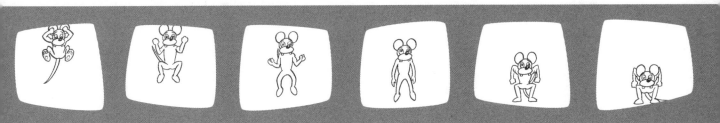

Head turn

We'll get around to hair, eyebrows, goatees, etc. in a moment. For now, let's turn what we've got for a three-quarter view.

1. Draw your oval again, with the same line lengthwise. This time, the center line is not only going to move, it's going to follow the shape of the head.

2. Using this new line as your guide, put the eyes on either side as shown.

3. Now do the same for the nose, ears, and mouth.

Not too tough, was it? Now let's use these ideas to draw a head in any position we like.

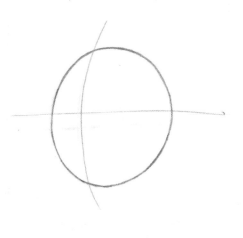

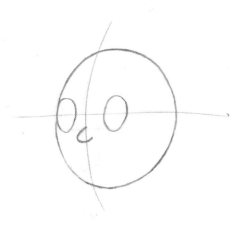

All angles covered

The dynamics of things

All of the images on this page use exactly the same principles as the previous pages.

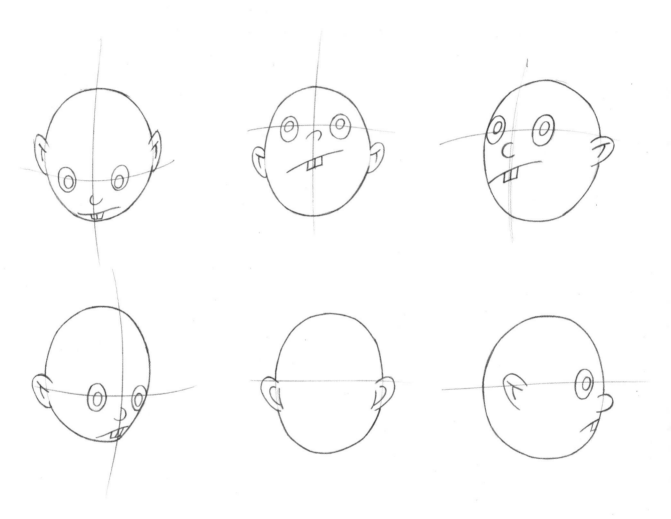

Pay close attention to the curve of your construction lines. Get these right and the facial features should be easy.

Let's get hairy

Even hair has some simple rules to follow. It doesn't just sprout out from anywhere. We don't need to get too carried away with detail and realism, but this map of human hair growth lets us get simple hair right every time.

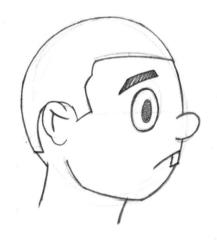

A feast of faces

Crazy 'bout d'em craniums

Now that we've got the basic head worked out, it's time to stretch out and go nuts. Try out some wild shapes to attach facial features to. See what works and what doesn't.

Animal heads

There's a major difference with animal heads. Most of them have some kind of muzzle or snout. This can be represented by an oval placed at this position.

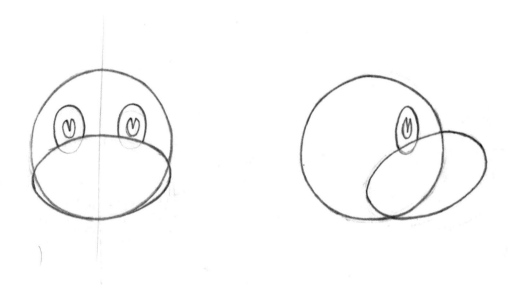

Here it is again, but this time much smaller and at a three-quarter angle.

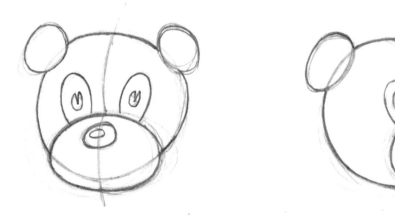

Now let's see what we can do with this information.

Hands

The enemy of the beginner

It needn't be hell. But for most people starting out, hands present the biggest problem of any part of the body. Some people can draw amazing cartoons, only to have the hands let them down by looking like bananas, or the victim of some bizarre turnip-sorting accident.

WHY DOES IT ALWAYS HAVE TO BE LIKE THIS?

So why are they so tough? Partly, it's because they're not one thing, but a collection of three things. We need to understand how the individual parts are constructed and work. They are:
1. Palm
2. Fingers
3. Thumb

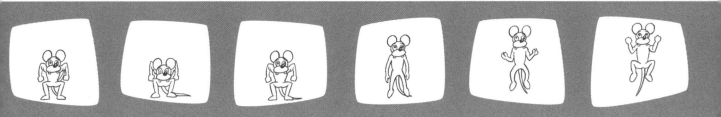

The palm

The palm is not going to present too much difficulty for us. But what shape? It needs a top edge for the fingers to project from, and a side edge for the thumb.

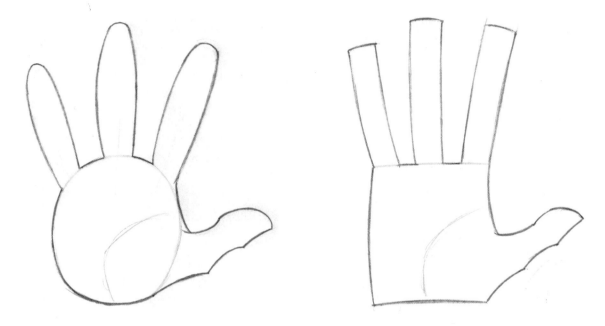

Let's go with the square type as it's more useful for this kind of instruction. Think of it as a slightly misshapen box.

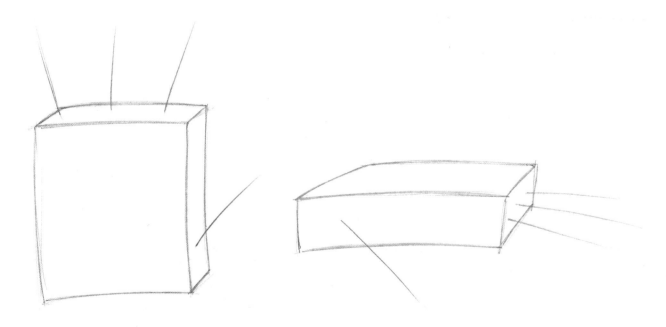

Finger and thumb placement

Now let's use this palm to map out the placement of the thumb and fingers. The all-important place to start is point A. Using this as a starting point, make an arc that swings up to point B. This arc marks out the area of the thumb. Next, starting at the same point, draw three straight lines, splaying out like a fan to C, D, and E. These represent the placement of the fingers. They do this by mimicking the position of our tendons. Check the back of your own hand to confirm this.

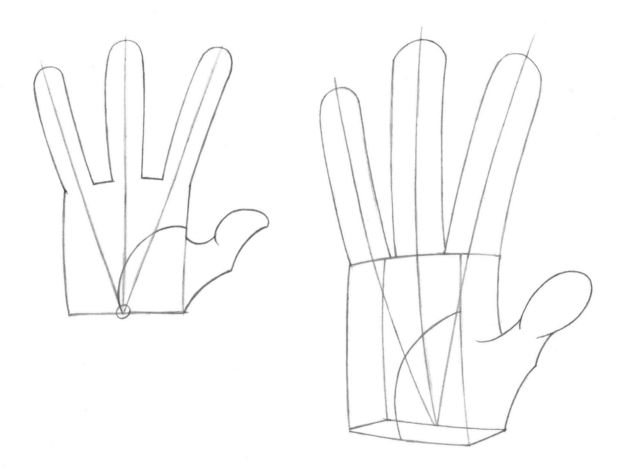

When we're happy with the result, we can then rotate the hand as shown to draw it in 3-D. Try drawing the palm box in any position you can imagine and then applying these principles. After doing this for long enough, you'll be able to get the position of the thumb and fingers without the need for mapping.

The three-fingered hand

You probably noticed there are only three fingers on this hand. You probably know most people have four. Long ago, at the dawn of cartoon time, someone realized you can be just as expressive with three fingers as with four. This means two things:
1. Simplicity (and thus strength) of expression.
2. A lot less work to do.

Intermission over. Back to the fingers.

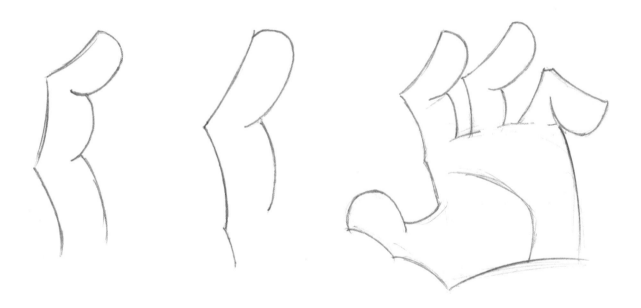

Although fingers have three joints, we don't always have to draw three joints. A two-jointed finger works fine for a lot of situations. If you look at the last chapter of this book, you'll see examples in the hand section that look as if they don't have joints at all. Whatever serves the need of the drawing is the rule here.

Knuckle sandwich

Let's take what we've already got and add some knuckle knowledge. The knuckles are pivotal points for expression. If we always know where these are in the hand, it's nearly impossible to get it wrong.

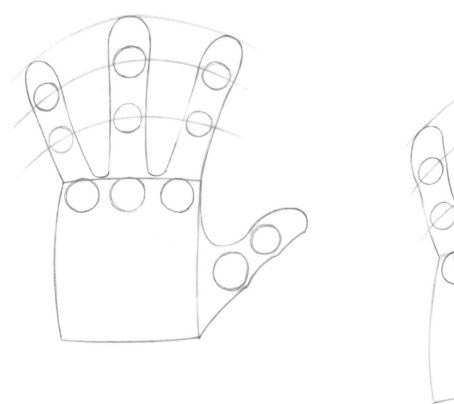

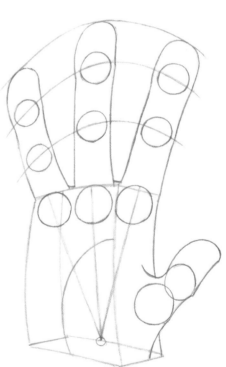

Again, if we're happy with the front view, let's turn it and draw the more difficult three-quarter view. The arcs are not symmetrical. They reflect the difference in size of the fingers, i.e. smallest, biggest, middle-sized.

All angles covered

Let's draw a cartoon classic hand position: the point

1. It's a side view, so we start with the palm in that position.

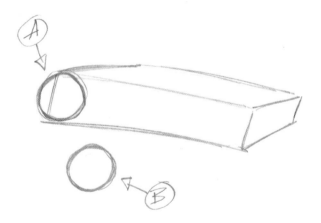

2. Add the knuckle of the forefinger at point A. Then add the major knuckle of the thumb at point B. That's the hardest part done.

3. Put the minor thumb knuckle in as shown and join the knuckles up. Add the tip of the thumb. Roughly indicate the position of the forefinger.

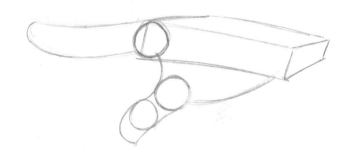

Pointing hand continued

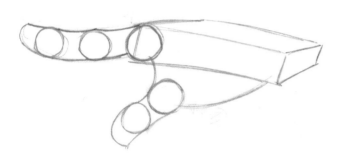

4. Show the position of the knuckles of the forefinger. Use these to make the finger shape more expressive.

5. Now put in the middle finger knuckle as shown. From this, draw the first joint of the middle finger. Now add the second joint, tucking it in under the major joint of the thumb.

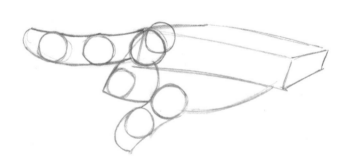

6. Put in the fold of the middle finger joint and generally firm everything up.

All done.

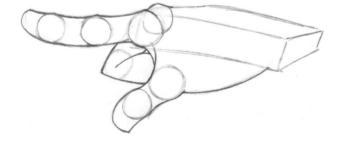

Maps of the human hand

To round off our section on hands, here's a few in various positions, showing the mapping. Remember, if your hands are going somewhere unpleasant in a hurry, simplify and map. It'll get you out of trouble every time.

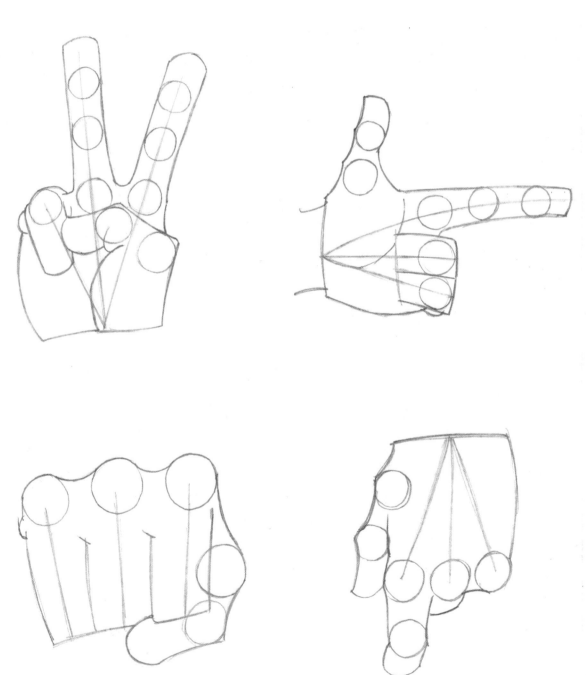

Feet

Not as hard as hands?

Because I never considered feet to be anywhere near as difficult as hands, my understanding of them dragged behind for years. But feet can be tough. Your character can be standing there brilliantly drawn. But what's this? He looks like he's about to keel over backwards. Or, he may look like he has two left feet or sprained ankles. And so on. To avoid any of the above, let's look at feet in their most basic construction.

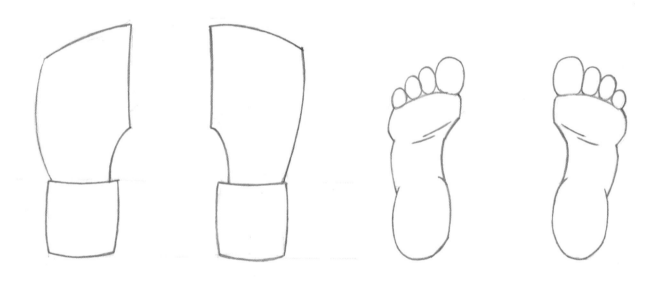

Top left shows the general shape of the feet. Compare this with the feet at top right.

Think of the foot as being divided into three sections: heel, arch, and toes.

The same basic shape applies to funny animal feet as well.

Other views of the feet

Most of the time, we don't have to draw the underside of the feet, so let's look at the more common positions.

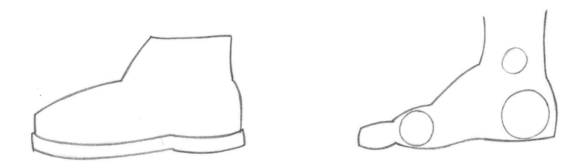

The joints we have to think about are the ankles and the knuckles of the toes. The heel isn't a joint as such but is the largest bone area.

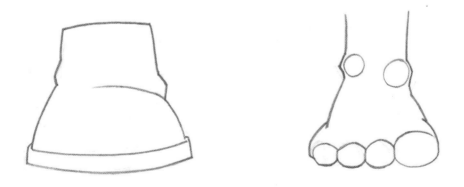

The ankle bones are good indicators of which foot (left or right) we are looking at, whether it's a naked foot, or a boot, or a shoe.

Podiatry in motion

Let's take a look at what happens when the foot bends. It will do this every time your character walks, kicks, or performs a triple salko, so there's no getting out of it.

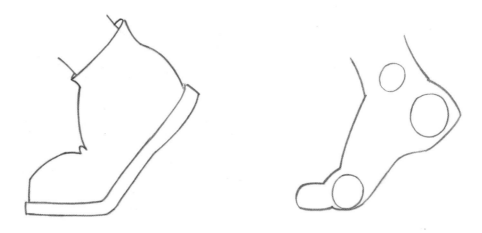

In the above drawing the toes stay in the same place. The rest of the foot pivots at the toe joint.

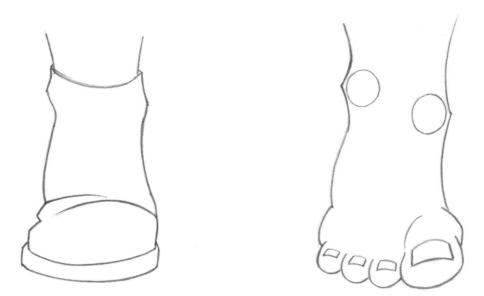

With the front view, it's the ankles again that are the most helpful in indicating the position of the foot, but the folds in the boot help a lot, too.

Enough with the technical stuff!

Let's get back to the fun stuff. Here's a page of what you might do with what we've just learned.

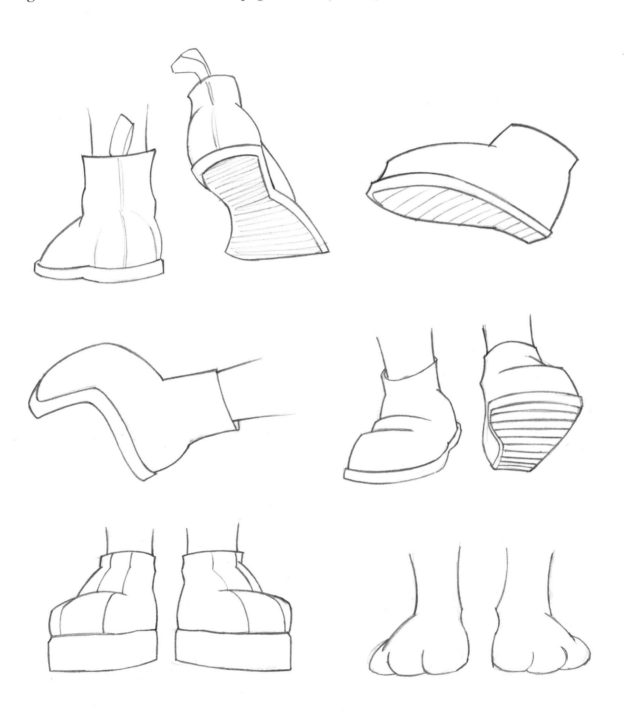

section four

cars and
buildings

Bricks and motors

Dressing the set

It's possible to create a cartoon strip without backgrounds or accessories, but let's face it, we need to draw this stuff.

We'll have a quick look at perspective and creating the illusion of depth, but to kick off this section, let's get a grip on transportation.

As with all objects, it's important to understand the *structure* of the thing we want to draw. This means breaking the object down to the simplest possible shapes. Only once we've done this and truly understood what's at the heart of any object can we then twist, mutate, stretch, and generally distort things to our own cartoon ends.

The following pages illustrate this idea. If you try to draw objects without keeping this in mind, your drawings will probably lack strength, or *structural integrity*. Shape *before* detail is the rule.

Let's get some wheels

Instant car recipe

There are only three things you need to put a basic cartoon car together. It may surprise you to know they can be found in your kitchen or bathroom.

Here's McCoon to show you.

– BAR OF SOAP (LARGE)   – PIE DISH (OBLONG)   – 4 × BOTTLE CAPS

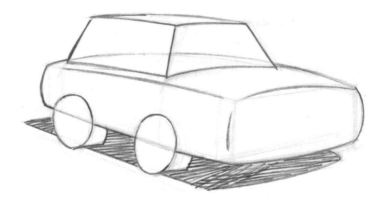

Put the pie dish upside down on top of the soap bar. Make sure you place it toward the back of the bar so you get a nice, big hood. Squish the bottle caps into the bottom half of the soap.

Soap-bar coupe

Add some features

Now that we've got the basics down, let's use this technique to create something with more horsepower.

1. Start by making another soap-bar shape.

2. Draw a line around the bar about one-third of the way back and another near the rear of the bar. These will represent the "cockpit" part of our car.

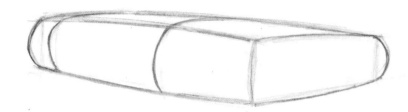

3. Put in the wheel arches as shown. Then add the windshield. Note the angles on the windshield are not the same.

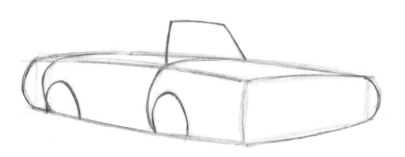

4. Now let's stick those bottle caps, sorry, wheels on. Let's go crazy and add some hub caps. Some seats would be handy, too.

5. Headlights, grille, fender, side mirrors, and antenna all go on now.

That's it! Pretty easy, eh?

Getting the most from your bar

Every car you can think of

Now that we understand the construction of our vehicle, we can have some fun drawing it in any position we want! How's this for a crazy angle?

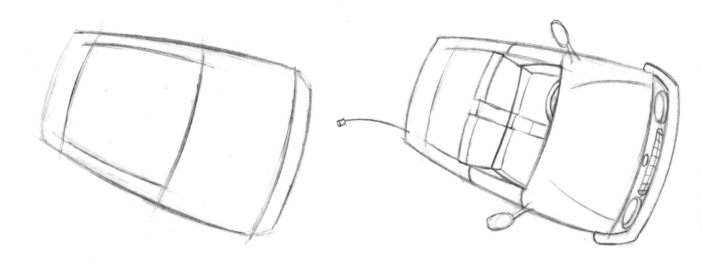

Stretch it

With all that under our belts, let's now create an array of different kinds of cars. The underlying construction will be exactly the same, but we'll push the limits to make some wilder shapes.

Building blocks

Structural engineering

Skyscrapers, salons, saloons, pizzerias, pie shops, and planetaria. Sooner or later we need to draw buildings. So what's stopping us? Probably knowing a few simple rules that make our panoramas plausible.

The one thing we need to get a handle on is perspective. Part physics and part perception, perspective not only helps make our cityscapes believable, it also allows us to get away with all kinds of visual stunts.

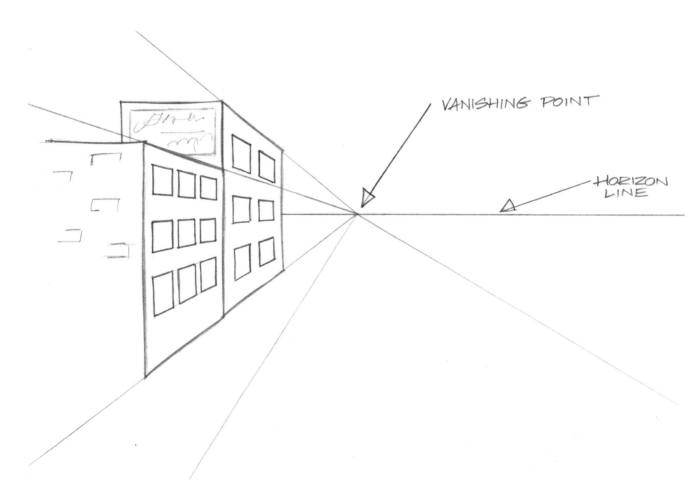

The above picture shows the most basic principles of perspective. The *horizon line* represents the line where the sky meets the land. In other words, as far as the eye can see. When something "disappears over the horizon," it does so at what is called the *vanishing point*. The diagonal lines which come from this point represent the correct angles at which to draw the horizontal lines of our buildings, roads, etc.

Civilization coming through!

Aaaahh . . . a beautiful, tranquil, rural scene. The bees are buzzing, the flowers blooming.
And not a building in sight, but all that's about to change.

The roadbuilders cometh

I used the rules of perspective three times in the above alteration. The obvious one is the road. Notice how it follows the arc of the bridge as it makes its way to the horizon line. The other two are the signpost and the paving bricks on the side road.

Industrial revolution

What our landscape really needs now is a couple of smokestacks belching out some good old-fashioned pollution. How about a bus shelter in the midground? And that riverside spot looks ideal for a plastics factory and a school.

Corporate development

Let's fell that old oak on the left and replace it with a big ugly office building. That antiquated road sign needs updating, too, and let's fence that last remaining greenery for a construction site.

Adding a restaurant

Now for some in-your-face perspective. We'll put up a new diner right where we stand. We can really see the perspective in action now. The diner's perspective lines were worked out with a ruler but finished freehand for an unmechanical look.

One-point perspective

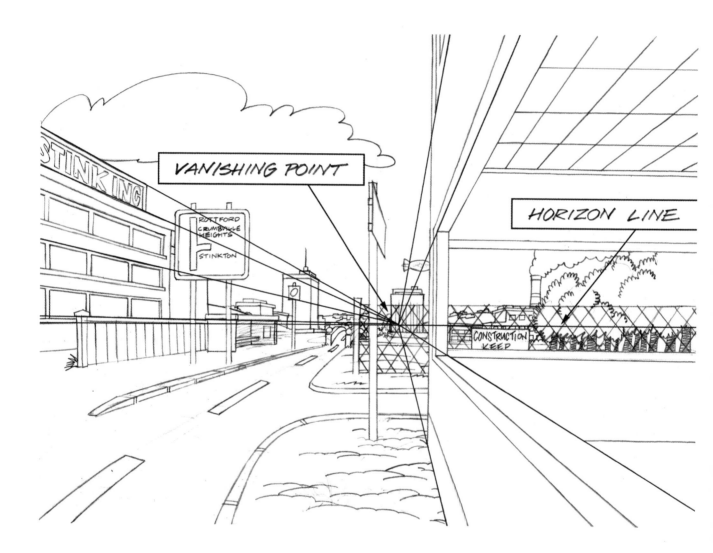

Here's the same image, this time showing the all-important perspective information. The angles on the buildings all lead to one single vanishing point. Note the hills in the background are above the horizon line.

More perspective

Greater depth

Now that we've got the basics of perspective under our belts, we'll look at creating more dramatic views. Have a look at the image below and see if you can tell how it differs technically from the one on the previous page.

As well as using the regular, horizontal perspective described earlier in this section, this drawing also uses *vertical* perspective. What this means is that things get smaller as they go downward, as well as toward the horizon line.

Of course, the effect is deliberately distorted in this image for greater effect. But imagine a point at the center of Earth; all vertical lines move toward this point.

Stage one

Planning

Before putting buildings or anything else in, we need to establish the perspective, both horizontal and vertical.

Put a horizon line in about four-fifths of the way up the page.

Choose a point on the horizon line to use for the general perspective of the buildings and streets. It's best not to make this dead center, as that can make the picture a little too symmetrical (and dull). Draw several vertical lines in a slight fan shape. These will act as guides for the vertical lines of our buildings. Put in a few random lines to the vanishing point, to suggest possible building locations.

Stage two

Blocking out time

We're going to have a street running toward the horizon line, so it's a good idea to indicate this first. This will also tell us where to put some of the buildings.

Now begin blocking out the shapes of the buildings, starting with those next to the street. Don't put any detail in at this stage, as you may well have to erase it again.

Stage three

Greater depth

Now that all the main buildings' positions have been established, we can work on the details and background. You can quickly build up loose background detail by drawing horizontal and vertical perspective lines close together and then allowing your imagination to fill in the gaps.

When you're happy with the buildings, you can add some traffic. Get some cars at street level and maybe a couple of blimps, and why not add flying saucers, too?

Stage four

Tighten up

If the loose drawings are to your liking, it's time to get them ready for the inks. This means making sure every line is strong and in the right place. For extra depth, ink the foreground with bolder strokes and the background with a slimmer line.

That's it for this chapter. By now, you should be able to draw some pretty decent backgrounds. Next up is the section that completes everything we need to know to assemble our own strips.

section five

create your own character

Create your own character

Starting from scratch

Whether we start with a doodle or begin with the character's personality depends largely on what we are trying to achieve. Does the character need to fit into an already existing scenario or world? Or will our character be the thing around which that world revolves?

For this book, I want to create a nemesis for a rodent character we'll meet later on in the book. I want this character to irritate the rodent, not deliberately, but just by going about his normal business. The character wouldn't have an ounce of malice in him but would unintentionally annoy the daylights out of Mr. Rodent.

The first thing we need to establish when coming up with a character is motivation. Why does he do the things he does? The list of possible motivations is nearly endless: greed, fear, love, boredom, curiosity, etc. But I wanted this character to be possessed of something insatiable that everyone can understand: hunger.

What kind of animal would fit the bill? Then it hit me. A perpetually hungry raccoon would wreak havoc on your trash cans and garden and would keep coming back until you found an appropriately permanent solution.

Doodling up

This was enough for a starting point. Other character aspects tend to show up along the way, so let's get going with this.

It's a good idea to just work up a few idle doodles to begin with. Let accidents happen, keep the good bits, and discard the parts that aren't working.

Below are the first doodles I did of the McCoon character.

The above right was the quickest, done in about 30—40 seconds, but it had something about it I liked. The final "look" of a character is often a hybrid of a bit of one drawing mixed with some aspect of another. McCoon is no exception.

Body stuff

Right physique for the character

We could choose an "off the rack" body type for our character. But it's more natural to experiment, doodle, and generally let characters evolve through the process of drawing them. I probably drew the McCoon character, or variations of him, around a hundred times before his face and body were fully settled and established.

On the drawing on the left, the head is way off, but I liked the general feel of the body shape and proportions, so I decided to run with this.

Now the head and body are starting to settle and feel right.

This is a good prototype to work with. I'll now draw him until my hand aches and see what changes occur.

Much later

Locking the character down

Now that the character is fully formed, we can start to think about applying some rules. By this I mean laying down guidelines to ensure that the character is always drawn consistently, no matter who draws him. Sometimes, while drawing a strip, storyboard, or whatever, our sense of a character can slip. The smallest differences can hugely alter the "feel" of the character. These nuances are often very subtle. This is where guidelines such as these are invaluable.

The next few pages are what are known as *model sheets*. They are used primarily in animation, but also in other visual arts where consistency of character is vitally important.

Even if you have no desire to animate your character or even make a full-blown comic strip with him, it's still incredibly good for your drawing abilities to create model sheets.

Knowing how any given character will look at any given angle adds a lot of strength to your ability to create.

"McCOON"

MODEL
SHEET
#1

"HEADS"

WHISKERS

3RD WHISKER
DOWN IS ALWAYS
LONGEST.

WHISKERS
"SWITCH" WHEN
HEAD TURNS
(SEE TURNAROUND)

NOSE

ALWAYS HAS
WHITE HIGHLIGHT,
EVEN IN DARK!

EYES

USE WHITE
SLITS WHEN
EYES ARE SHUT.

EARS

ARE SQUARED
OFF - NEVER
ROUND.

ATTACH
TO HEAD
WITH THIS
SHAPE.

MOUTH

UPPER LIP
CAN "SWITCH"

IN PROFILE,
SHOW PROTRUSION
OF LOWER LIP.

"McCOON"

MODEL
SHEET
#2

"EXPRESSION"

NO EYEBROWS –
USE EYEPATCHES TO
CREATE REACTIONS

DROOP EARS
& WHISKERS
WHEN WET,
CRESTFALLEN,
TIRED ETC.

"JUST EATEN"

MOUTH OPENS
LIKE SO

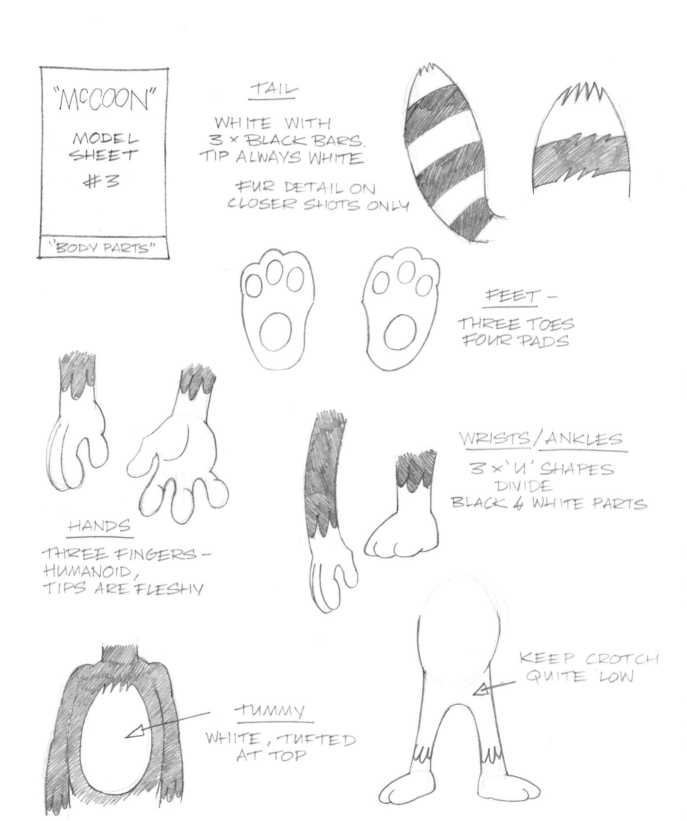

"McCOON"

MODEL
SHEET
#3

"BODY PARTS"

TAIL

WHITE WITH
3 × BLACK BARS.
TIP ALWAYS WHITE

FUR DETAIL ON
CLOSER SHOTS ONLY

FEET –
THREE TOES
FOUR PADS

HANDS

THREE FINGERS –
HUMANOID,
TIPS ARE FLESHY

WRISTS / ANKLES

3 × 'U' SHAPES
DIVIDE
BLACK & WHITE PARTS

TUMMY
WHITE, TUFTED
AT TOP

KEEP CROTCH
QUITE LOW

"McCOON"

MODEL SHEET #3

"BODY PARTS"

McCOON SNEAKS AROUND A LOT — TRYING TO GET PAST RATCHET'S SECURITY.

HE ALSO EATS A LOT — HAS A VERY EXPANDABLE TUMMY.

CLIMBS INTO TRASH CANS LIKE A CAT.

Turnarounds

But what does he look like in the rear three-quarter position

The images on these two pages are known as "turnarounds" or "character rotations." Their usefulness should be immediately apparent, as these show our character from all directions.

1.   2.   3.

Positions 7 and 8 are not shown, as these would be more or less identical to 3 and 2 but looking the opposite way. The top tier shows the character construction while the bottom tier shows the finished inked result.

4.   5.   6.

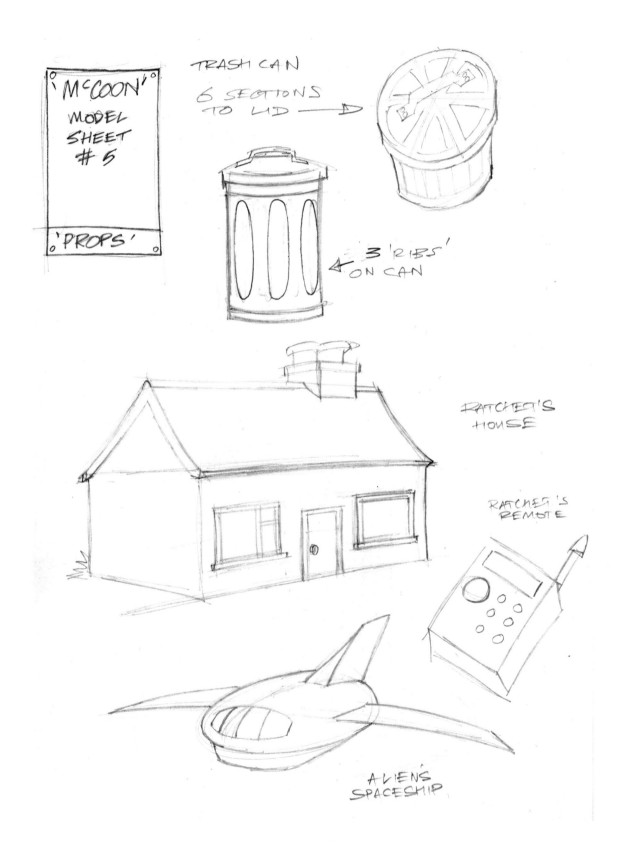

'McCOON'

MODEL SHEET #5

'PROPS'

TRASH CAN

6 SECTIONS TO LID

3 'RIBS' ON CAN

RATCHET'S HOUSE

RATCHET'S REMOTE

ALIEN'S SPACESHIP

Props

As well as all the information needed to keep a character consistent, any props, vehicles, etc. that appear also need to have model sheets. This is especially true of any animated show. These shows will have reams and reams of model sheets for absolutely everything of any importance, however fleeting their on-screen appearance. If it's going to be animated, it needs a model sheet. If it appears in a background more than once, it needs a model sheet.

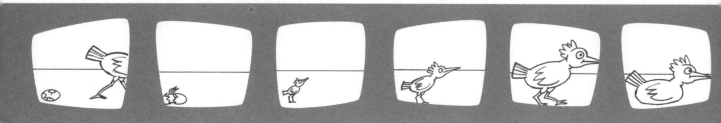

Chicken, egg, or raccoon?

Writing for your character

As I said earlier, story type depends on character type. Is the character serious or silly? Profound or profoundly stupid?

Here's a simple formula for plot development that works. Take two or three well-developed characters. Come up with a simple scenario. Put one of the characters in a difficult situation. Have the others react to that character's plight. It doesn't matter in the slightest if the scenario completely changes. If the characters are strong, they will almost write the script for you. If you know your characters, you'll know their reactions, their feelings, their motivations.

One of the biggest stumbling blocks to writing a script for your characters is the idea that you have to come up with a brilliant, fully formed script in your head before you do anything else. Not true. Nearly all your great ideas are going to come during the process of writing. Unexpected twists and turns will occur to you as your story unfolds.

There's a vast number of books on the subject of storytelling out there, probably too many to read in a lifetime. These are a great source of ideas about storytelling, many of which have come down to us from as long ago as the time of the ancient Greeks. Archetypes, plots, subplots, heroes, antiheroes if you're serious about storytelling, get yourself down to your local library or bookstore. It'll help you get a grip on the mechanics of what makes a story work.

Ready for action

Well, almost

I mentioned earlier that aspects of a character have a habit of presenting themselves during the process of development. I've now got a better idea of who this character is and have added some more detail to flesh him out.

There are two more things we need to work on, both coming up in the next section. Then we can put it all together and make a complete comic strip.

section six

effects and finishes

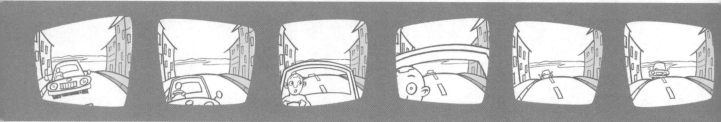

Boom, crash, zang

Adding sound to a piece of paper

Where would comic strips be without sound? An explosion without a "boom" is like a pig without an "oink." These examples of onomatopoeia work partly by their dynamism. What I mean is, they communicate the *idea* of the sound. Here's what I mean.

Above are two pictures of a standard cartoon explosion. The one on the left has perfectly funtional lettering. Functional and boring. The image on the right does the job with way more impact. The letters are being blown off the page!

Visual sounds

Below is a sampling of several different sounds appropriate for a variety of different situations. You should be able to get an idea of what they may be used for, not just from their sound but also from the way they *look*.

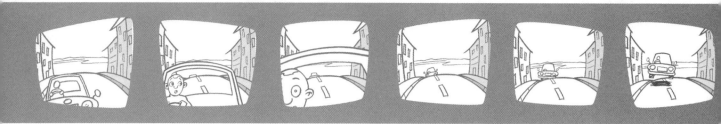

Full throttle

Speed lines, and other attention grabbers

Anyone familiar with comic strips the world over should be familiar with speed lines. They are the trail left by characters, vehicles, etc. on the move. To an extent they are an attempt to mimic the motion blur in photographs caused by the film speed being too slow for the subject, often deliberately.

Below is an everyday scene of a rat riding a high-speed missile. The image below is perfectly serviceable; you know the direction the missile is traveling and you get some idea of speed.

ERR....
FINE, I
SUPPOSE.

But come on! This is a missile we're talking about. It has to have the kind of speed that would threaten to tear the whiskers off your face! Let's try again.

YEAH!
FEEL THAT
WIND IN
YOUR FACE!

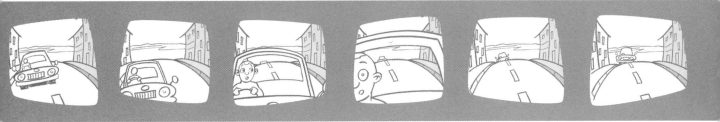

Hey! Over here!

Another device that exists purely to add drama or focus attention is the *aura*. The sudden appearance of an important character, the discovery of some important item, or a character in a state of shock, these are all common uses of the aura. By surrounding the object of our attention with this device, the eye has little choice but to focus on it.

LINES: These are similar to speed lines. The main difference is that they never come into contact with the person or object. The idea is to create a kind of glow around the point of focus.

ABSTRACT SHAPES: As with the lines, leave empty space to produce the "glow" effect. This technique, pioneered by the great Jack Kirby, is great for evil or extra-powerful characters.

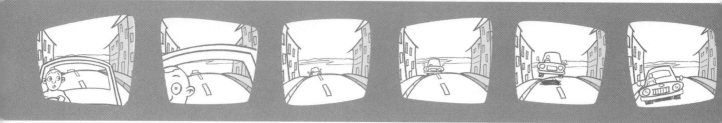

Making it permanent

Using inks for finished artwork

In section one I mentioned the options available to us to ink our work. The ideas here are general and applicable no matter what kind of black juice you use to finalize your artwork.

Why ink at all?
Certainly, no one is forcing you to. You might be happy with just penciling. Comic books and strips often have separate people for both pencils and inks. But anyone who has to get their artwork ready for production and doesn't have a reliable ink artist at hand is going to need to know something about this art.

And it is an art. However, the legendary Superman/Lois Lane artist Kurt Schaffenberger once said: "It's a job that any well-trained orangutan should be able to do. There's nothing creative about it, particularly." This caused shock and disbelief among many. How can he say this? It's a no-brainer that a bad inker can wreck a good penciler's work, just as a brilliant inker can salvage the dullest pencils, at least to some considerable extent.

Schaffenberger's pencils were *so* tight and *so* polished, they allowed little room for an inker's creativity. It may have been true of *his* pencils that anyone could ink them, but this is very much the exception, not the rule.

AND THEY SAID THIS WAS HARD!

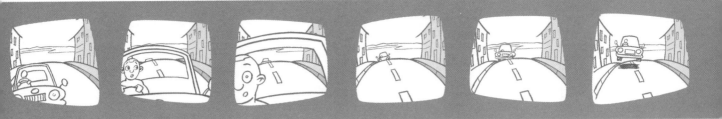

Ink this!

Pre-prepared pencils prior to permanent pigmentation

Below is a scene penciled and ready to be inked. There's not only a choice of brush, pen, or marker, there's also the choice of style and approach. Tight, loose, heavy, or light, or a combination of all of these.

Before turning the page, have a good look at the above picture and imagine how you might ink this piece yourself. Then look overleaf and see if you see anything like you imagined . . . .

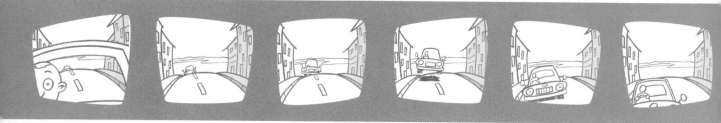

Tight brush inks

The version below has been inked with a brush and India ink. The number one and number two brushes were heavily loaded with ink to give a slick, hard line.

The image contains all the foreground, midground, and background elements to enable us to create a feeling of depth. This is easily achieved with a brush, as it allows us to make a wide variety of stroke widths, depending on the pressure we apply to the brush.

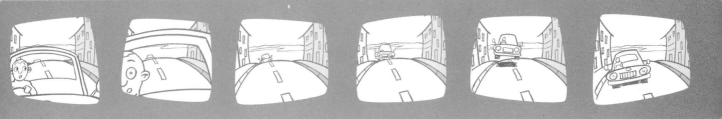

A looser approach

This version has been inked in a faster, less technical way. Although it lacks the tightness typical of animation, it does have more energy and life.

Even more than the last image, this approach requires plenty of ink in the brush or pen. Running out of ink halfway through a long line would probably be disastrous. It's almost impossible to fix up a "fast" brush line in a way that looks convincing. This method requires more confidence than the previous page, but if you can pull it off, the results can be great.

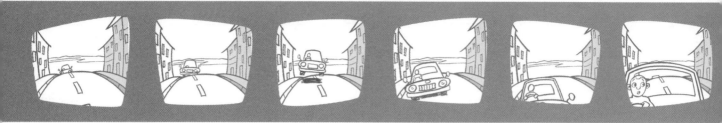

Marker pen

A marker pen can be a good choice to ink with. It dries almost immediately, it's easier to control, and the results can be pretty distinctive. The downside is the ink isn't that black and can turn gray once you erase. Also, it requires the use of bleedproof paper to prevent "fuzziness" due to the solvent content.

Try experimenting with all of the above approaches. Even if you don't like the results, you'll find out what you don't like, and that can often be just as important.

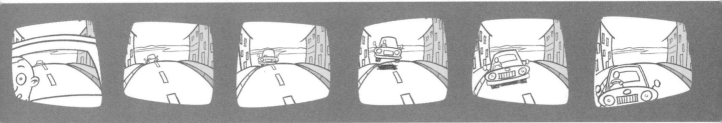

How to get it wrong

It can be just as informative to show how to ink badly as well as decently. I therefore present to you a visual catalog of how not to do it. The image below features inking mistakes and is intended to serve as a warning of possible pitfalls. See how many glaring errors and bad ideas you can spot!

Some ways to avoid the above happening to you:

1. Never ink near work you're not sure is bone dry, to avoid big, ugly smudges.
2. Don't start inking before the pencils are totally finished.
3. Focus attention on what's important, not the background.
4. Use heavy lines for foreground, lighter as the scene recedes.
5. Leave any large areas of black until last.
6. Be consistent.

section seven

strips!

Draw your own strip!

Making a story work

We've now covered all the elements needed to put our own strip together. We've created the characters, we know how to draw the background and effects, and speech bubbles are now second nature to us.

But what about a story?

To a large extent, the characters we've created will dictate the kind of story we are likely to tell. Having Ratchet and McCoon sitting around discussing geometric theorems would not only be boring, it would be inappropriate.

These two characters are from the "classic" template discussed earlier in the book. Hijinks, misadventure, and rascally behavior are the bread and butter of their existence. So let's put them in a situation that allows them to do what they do best.

Read on.

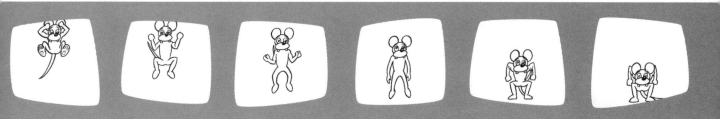

SO HUNGRY. . . AND NO NEW GARBAGE IN RATCH'S CANS FOR DAYS!

EGAD! NOTHING! MUST BE IN CAN NUMBER TWO - I CAN SMELL IT!

BINGO! FRESH TRASH!

SURELY HE MEANS "FRESH TRAP!"

THAT RATCH IS *NUTS!* THIS SPANISH OMELET'S HARDLY BEEN TOUCHED!

THAT WAS GREAT! ≈BELCH≈ TIME FOR FORTY WINKS BEFORE DAWN...

GOOD-BYE, McCOON — HELLO, SHINY NEW TRASH CAN!

AAAHH...AND A SHOOTING STAR...

OH, NO.

NO, NO, NO.

IT CAN'T POSSIB—

BLANG

≈YAWN≈ MORNING, RATCH. WHAT HAPPENED TO YOU?

HO, HO.

Breakdowns

No, not the nervous kind. A breakdown is the initial stage of arranging all the elements in each panel.

The main points we need to consider before doing this are:

1. Number of pages/panels needed to tell the story.
2. Character and background positions.
3. Keeping the reader interested.

This, obviously, requires a certain amount of planning. Before using our nice, high-quality paper, it's a good idea to do what are called "thumbnails." This has nothing to do with pedicures and everything to do with planning.

Use any old piece of scrap paper for this. It only needs to be big enough so you can see what's going on. Use this to *very roughly* work out your layout ideas. Remember, the only person who needs to understand these thumbnails is you, so work quickly and don't be fussy.

Page 1 breakdowns

PANEL 1 is what's known as the establishing shot, or "splash." As the first name implies, it's where we establish the location of our action, as well as the characters in it.

We need to set the scene, so let's draw not just the outside of Ratchet's house, but also some surrounding area. It's a typical cartoon suburban scene.

PANEL 2 shows McCoon having moved from the fence to reach Ratch's oh-so-tempting trash cans.

If it wasn't totally clear from PANEL 1, then PANEL 3 shows beyond doubt that Ratchet knows exactly what McCoon is up to.

Through the magic of cartoons, we have jumped from outside the house into Ratchet's front room!

Page 2

In PANEL 1 we've shown the remote handset in Ratchet's hand on the previous page. Now we'll give the reader a ringside seat to see what happens when Ratchet presses that button. This view allows the best view of both characters.

PANEL 2 shows the power involved in Ratchet's trap. McCoon has left Earth and is traveling into deep space.

PANEL 3 shows just how far he has traveled. Nonetheless, he is still completely oblivious to the alien spaceship, being more interested in the food available in the trash can.

PANEL 4 gives us an inside view of the aliens' ship. We only have one panel for characterization, so let's make it a keen young thing/jaded old commander theme, just for laughs.

PANEL 5 needs to show the trash can blasted back toward Earth.

116

Page 3

PANEL 1 is the first real close-up of the trash can hurtling back through space. McCoon is finishing his meal.

As we've seen nothing of McCoon himself for more than a page, let's have a peek inside the trash can in PANEL 2. We cut back to Ratchet's home for PANEL 3. This time, though, we'll use an overhead shot. This will show us all the elements we need. The location, the "shooting star," and Ratchet's position all need to be shown.

PANEL 4 is a close-up realization and reaction shot. Ratchet and McCoon are dramatically reunited here, so we need to get maximum impact from this panel.

PANEL 5 wraps the strip up, showing us the consequences of Ratchet's doomed attempts to get rid of McCoon.

117

Finishing pencils

Tightening up

When we're happy with the basic layout, and we've made any changes necessary, we can sharpen up a darker pencil and finalize the drawing.

When I was working on newspaper strips back in the dark ages of the 1990s, I had to handwrite every bit of lettering. These days, a great deal of the lettering is taken care of by the use of computer fonts. For this strip, I used handlettering to establish the dialogue on the roughs, then used a computer to do the finished typeface.

It's worth practicing your handlettering, even if you do have access to a good computer. It will give you a good understanding of what works and what doesn't, and why. Even though the handlettering on these roughs is hastily laid down and only half legible, it is consistent. This means I know that when it comes to the computer's job, all the words are going to fit!

Page 1

Firstly, we need to add in the character names and title on PANEL 1. This is usually superimposed on a computer, but for the benefit of those without technology, I'm doing it the old-school way straight on top of the artwork.

When we've done that, the next job is tightening up the speech balloons. We may as well do the whole page at once.

With the titles and balloons in place, we now know exactly how much room we have for the actual artwork. We can now finish the detail, too. Compare the above with the breakdown to see how much needs adding to our final drawing. The last thing you should put in are the black areas. Putting these in earlier will result in a very "smudgy" and potentially confusing final drawing.

Page 2

There's a whole host of detail to add on this page, especially on the spaceship interior. Again, though, you should begin with the speech balloons and also the effects noises.

A note about the stars. I've put these directly on the page to be inked around. This has to be the most time-consuming method possible! A better way, even if you don't have a computer, is to get some very opaque white paint and add them when you've inked in all the black area. Much quicker, much tidier.

For those of you with a computer, just use several different sized brushes set to pure white to create your star field.

Page 3

This final page uses a wide variety of scenes. This is partly because the story requires it, but also to create the maximum visual interest on the page.

Compare PANELS 3 and 4. The first is a "long shot," the second a close-up. It's as if we've zoomed right in from above, into Ratchet's horrified face. The line thickness on this panel is very heavy. Line thickness plays a big part in conveying distance. This page more than the others should make this clear.

With all the drawings now worked out, it's time to get out those inks and finish the job. Compare these penciled pages with the final versions. The inked version is more polished, but there are essentially no major differences to the actual artwork.

In conclusion

I said toward the end of the last section that developing these characters and story led me to some more ideas about Ratchet and McCoon. Here's the complete skinny on these two miscreants.

McCoon:
He is perpetually after freshly filled trash cans to rifle through, especially if they belong to his "friend" Ratchet. In addition to being almost permanently hungry, he appears to be just a little bit brainless. In reality, he's simply *as smart as he needs to be.* This is compounded by a simple but important fact: He happens to be the luckiest raccoon on the planet. This leads Ratchet to devise increasingly devious and escape-proof traps to foil McCoon with.

Ratchet:
Seemingly way smarter than McCoon, this rodent has both a technology degree and a huge ego. He longs to prove his cleverness by using his understanding to make the ultimate trap for McCoon. This plan can never come off, as Ratchet refuses to factor in the one thing that always saves McCoon dumb luck.

Those aliens:
The Boredomians endlessly travel the universe, simply because their own planet is so incredibly dull. They have been everywhere and seen everything. Trying to get any genuine interest out of a Boredomian is tougher than getting rid of McCoon.

section eight

reference

Reference material

When you're stuck

The following pages are supplementary material. If you're truly stuck for a pose, or just can't figure out why those hands look so wrong, this could be the place to turn.

I've tried to include as wide a cross-section of useful material as possible, such as hands in everyday and not-so-everyday poses and grips, humans, animals, and anthropomorphic types doing what they do best.

Rounding off the chapter, and the book, is a quick look at how the cover that adorns this publication was created.

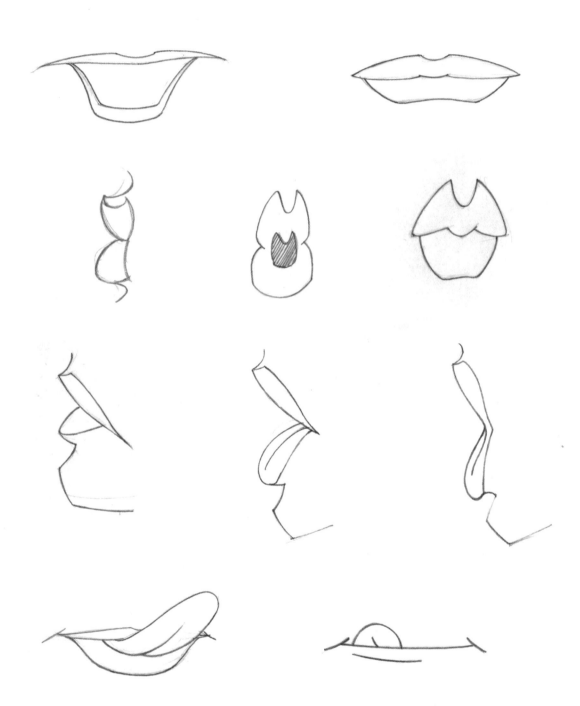

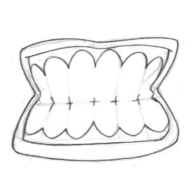
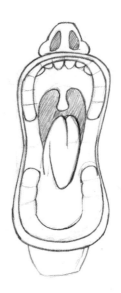

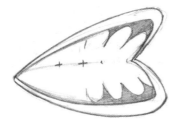
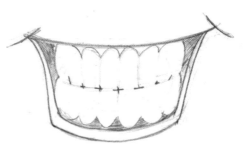

USING EYELIDS & EYEBROWS TO CONVEY EMOTION

RELAXED

WORRIED

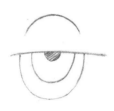

TIRED

SURPRISED

EXHAUSTED

HAPPY

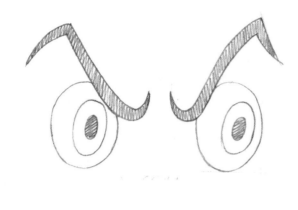

ANGRY

CRAZED

LOVESTRUCK

STOOPID

MINEFIELD

How the cover of this book was made

When putting together an important image such as a book cover, there are several stages in its development.

The two images on this page are both "roughs" little more than doodles at this stage.

At left is my preliminary sketch of the cover idea. As you can see, I'd already decided on the character types I wanted to use (the classic dog, cat, and mouse). The next stage was to arrange the elements into a strong composition.

The image above has some good points, but also a few which I felt were not quite working or were inappropriate. Both the dog and cat look too evil, when what I really wanted was "silly." Also, the diagonal design leaves too many "weak spots" areas that don't serve any purpose.

On the right are the three characters arranged in more of a "triangle" pattern. This gives our image a stronger structure.

Now, we're getting close to the finished final drawing.

Above is the drawing that was used to create the final inked image for the cover. I decided to lose the cutlery idea it was good, but was spoiling the design a little. I also chose a more mild-mannered-looking dog (apart from the huge mallet he's holding). This provides more contrast with the crazed cat.

On the right is the inked image just prior to having color applied.

This image was then applied over the montage background before finally adding the text.

Hey, presto one book cover!